FAVOURITE
RETRO
RECIPES

Illustrated with
nostalgic kitchen images from
the 1950s and 1960s

SALMON

Index

Avocado Dip   10

Beef Provençale   38

Beef Stroganoff   35

Chicken Chasseur   24

Chicken Kiev   21

Chicken Maryland   22

Chicken with Pineapple   23

Chilli con Carne   31

Chocolate Roulade   46

Coronation Chicken   26

Cottage Cheese & Pineapple Dip   10

Crêpes Suzette   42

Crispy Corned Tuna   16

Duck with Orange Sauce   27

French Onion Soup   5

Gazpacho   6

Lasagne   34

Lemon Cheesecake   43

Lemon Meringue Pie   39

Moussaka   32

Mushrooms à la Grecque   7

Pineapple Upside-down Pudding   40

Prawn Cocktail   8

Quiche Lorraine   11

Raspberry Ripple Ice Cream   45

Scampi Provençale   14

Salmon Mousse   15

Sherry Trifle   47

Spanish Omelette   13

Steak Diane   37

Trout with Almonds   18

Turkey à la King   19

Veal Marsala   30

Vichyssoise   3

Wiener Schnitzel   29

Kitchen images sourced from The History of Advertising Trust Archive
www.hatads.org.uk.
Printed and published by J. Salmon Ltd., Sevenoaks, England © Copyright

Vichyssoise

2 leeks	¾ pint chicken stock
1 oz. butter	Salt
1 onion, thinly sliced	Freshly ground black pepper
8 oz. potatoes, diced	6 tablespoons single cream

Thinly slice the leeks. Melt the butter in a saucepan and add the leek and onion.
Fry gently until soft but not coloured. Add the potatoes and stock, season to taste
and bring to the boil. Cover and simmer gently for about 30 minutes until the
vegetables are tender. Cool slightly, liquidise the soup and return to a clean
saucepan. Stir the cream gradually into the soup and reheat gently to just below
boiling point and adjust the seasoning. Allow to cool, then chill thoroughly.

French Onion Soup

4 medium onions, finely sliced   1½ pints beef stock
2 oz. butter   1 clove garlic, crushed
2 oz. grated cheese (Cheddar, Gruyère or any hard cheese)
1 stick French bread   Sherry (optional)
Salt and pepper

Melt the butter in a heavy bottomed saucepan and gently fry the onions and crushed garlic until a light golden colour. Add the beef stock and a dash of sherry (if required). Season to taste and cook for about 30 minutes until the onions are well softened. Slice the French bread and lightly toast under a grill. Spread grated cheese on each slice, return to the grill until the cheese is melted and the bread fully toasted. Serve the soup in bowls with one or more slices of bread on top of the soup.

Gazpacho

1lb. tomatoes, skinned	3 slices fresh white bread
1 medium cucumber	1 tablespoon red wine vinegar
1 medium onion	2 tablespoons olive oil
1 medium red pepper, deseeded	10 fl.oz. tomato juice
1 medium green pepper, deseeded	10 fl.oz. cold water
1 clove garlic, crushed	Salt and pepper

Roughly chop the onion and half of the cucumber and the peppers. Put these and all the other ingredients into a blender and blend until smooth. Season to taste. Serve well chilled in individual soup bowls with an ice cube in each. Garnish with the remainder of the cucumber and peppers, finely chopped, and sprinkle with small bread croutons.

Mushrooms à la Grecque

2 tablespoons olive oil   1 medium onion, finely chopped
2 cloves garlic, crushed   2 level tablespoons tomato purée
½ pint red wine   Bouquet garni
1 tablespoon coriander seeds, lightly crushed
1 level teaspoon sugar   Salt and pepper
1 lb. button mushrooms
8 oz. tomatoes, skinned, quartered and seeded
Chopped fresh coriander, to garnish

Heat the oil in a large frying pan, add the onion and garlic and cook gently for 5 minutes. Stir in the tomato purée, wine, bouquet garni, coriander seeds, sugar and seasoning. Add the mushrooms and tomatoes and cook gently, uncovered, for about 10 minutes, until all the vegetables are just tender. Remove the bouquet garni and spoon the mushrooms and cooking liquid into a serving dish. Chill well and serve sprinkled with coriander. Serves 4.

Prawn Cocktail

½ round lettuce, washed and dried
4 tablespoons plain yogurt
2 tablespoons mayonnaise
2 tablespoons Worcestershire sauce

3 tablespoons tomato ketchup
2 level teaspoons horseradish sauce
2 tablespoons lemon juice
8 oz. peeled prawns

Shred lettuce and use to half-fill four large wine glasses. Set aside. Combine the mayonnaise with the yogurt, ketchup, Worcestershire and horseradish sauces and lemon juice. Add prawns and mix well. Chill lightly. Spoon equal amounts into glasses. Serve with thinly sliced brown bread and butter.

Cottage Cheese & Pineapple Dip

4 tablespoons soured cream   8 oz. cottage cheese
4 heaped tablespoons canned pineapple, finely chopped
Salt   Cayenne pepper
Red and/or green peppers, chopped

Mix the cottage cheese with the soured cream and pineapple. Season to taste with salt and a little cayenne pepper. Transfer to a bowl and garnish with red or green peppers, or a mixture of both.

Avocado Dip

8 oz. cream cheese   1 tablespoon onion, finely grated
4 tablespoons mayonnaise   2 tablespoons parsley, chopped
$\frac{1}{4}$ pint fresh double cream   1 clove of garlic, crushed
1 avocado pear, mashed   Salt and pepper

Beat the cream cheese with the mayonnaise until smooth. Lightly whip the cream, and stir into the cheese mixture. Mix in remaining ingredients. Transfer to a bowl for serving.

Quiche Lorraine

6 oz. shortcrust pastry ¼ pint milk
4 oz. streaky bacon 3 standard eggs, beaten
¼ pint fresh single cream Salt and pepper
Large pinch grated nutmeg

Roll out the pastry and line an 8 inch baking tin. Cut the bacon into strips and fry lightly until soft but not crisp. Dry on soft kitchen paper to remove any excess fat. Line base of pastry case with the bacon. Heat the milk and cream to just below boiling point and combine with the beaten eggs. Season with grated nutmeg and salt and pepper to taste. Pour into the pastry case and bake in centre of moderately hot oven, 400°F or Mark 6 for 10 minutes. Reduce the temperature to moderate 325°F or Mark 3. Bake for further 35 to 45 minutes until filling is set. Serve hot.

Spanish Omelette

4 eggs, beaten
About 2 medium size potatoes or a few small new potatoes
3 tablespoons olive oil   1 onion, chopped   1 clove of garlic, chopped

Peel or scrub the potatoes and slice thinly. Heat 2 tablespoons of oil in a large frying pan. Put the potato slices in the pan with the onion and garlic. Cover the pan and cook until the potatoes are tender, turning them occasionally. Beat the eggs lightly in a large bowl. When the potato and onion mixture is cooked, add it to the bowl and mix together. Put the other tablespoon of oil in the pan and turn the heat down as low as it will go. Pour the egg, onion and potato mixture into the pan. The essence of this dish is slow cooking and it should take about 20 minutes. When there is little liquid left, turn the omelette over. It should need about another 2 minutes cooking. Or, to avoid having to turn the contents of the pan over, and if a grill is available, sprinkle some grated cheese on the surface of the omelette and put the pan under the grill until the omelette is golden brown on top.

In addition to potato and onion, many other vegetables may be added, as preferred, i.e. tomatoes, mushrooms, peppers, peas, etc. Chop them as appropriate and add to the pan after the onion and potato have fried for a little while.

Scampi Provençale

1 oz. butter
1 medium onion, finely chopped
1 garlic clove, finely chopped
14 oz. can tomatoes, drained

6 tablespoons dry white wine
Salt and pepper
1 tablespoon fresh parsley, chopped
1 lb. frozen scampi, thawed and drained

Heat the butter in a saucepan, add the onion and garlic and fry gently for about 5 minutes, until soft but not coloured. Add the tomatoes, wine, seasoning and parsley, stir well and simmer gently for about 10 minutes. Add the scampi and continue simmering for about 5 minutes, or until they are just heated through. Serve with crusty French bread.

Salmon Mousse

1 lb. fresh salmon
Bunch fresh herbs or bouquet garni
½ pint double cream
2 oz. butter

4 fl.oz. dry sherry
2 tablespoons lemon juice
Salt and pepper
½ oz. powdered gelatine

Set oven to 350°F or Mark 4. Lightly oil a 1 lb loaf tin or a salmon mould. Place the salmon in a buttered ovenproof dish with the fresh herbs and cover with water. Cover the dish with foil and cook for 20 minutes. Leave the salmon to cool in the liquid, then remove the skin and bones, but reserve the liquid. Pound the salmon until smooth. Lightly whip the cream and fold into the salmon. Soften the butter and stir into the mixture together with the sherry and lemon juice. Season to taste. Measure 6 tablespoons of the reserved fish liquid into a bowl and sprinkle the gelatine on top. Set over a pan of hot water until the gelatine has dissolved. Cool slightly and then beat into the mousse. Spoon the mousse into the tin or mould and leave to set in the refrigerator overnight. Serve either turned out on to a serving dish or straight from the tin.

Crispy Corned Tuna

1 oz. butter   1 oz. flour   ½ pint milk
2 oz. Cheddar cheese, grated
Salt and freshly ground black pepper
1 x 7 oz./200 gram can tuna, drained
1 x 11½ oz./400 gram can sweetcorn, drained
2 large tomatoes, finely sliced

Melt the butter in a saucepan. Stir in the flour and cook for 1 minute. Gradually add the milk and bring to the boil, stirring constantly. Simmer for 2 minutes, stir in the cheese and season to taste. Flake the tuna and add to the sauce. Fold in the sweetcorn. Line a greased ovenproof dish with the tomato slices. Spoon the tuna mixture into the centre of the dish. Place in a moderate oven 350°F or Mark 4 for about 20 minutes, until the top is brown and crisp. Delicious served with thick slices of French bread.

Trout with Almonds

4 trout (small ones are quite good for this recipe)
4 oz. butter   4 oz. almonds, flaked
Seasoned flour   Lemon juice

Wash and clean the trout and pat dry. Rub all over with the flour until coated. Heat the butter in a pan until it is bubbling and fry the trout 4-5 minutes on each side. When ready, put in a dish to keep hot. Add more butter to the pan if necessary and fry the almonds until golden brown, no more. Cover the fish evenly with the almonds and keep warm. Add the juice of a large lemon to the butter which the fish and almonds were cooked in and just bring to the boil. Pour over the fish at once. Serve in a dish garnished with fresh parsley. The nice thing about fried trout is that the skin is so delicious and it is a pleasure to eat it when crispy and golden.

Turkey à la King

2 oz. butter	1 lb. cooked turkey meat, diced
1 green pepper, chopped	Salt and pepper
4 oz. mushrooms, sliced	Paprika
2 oz. flour	Grated nutmeg
1 pint milk	1-2 tablespoons sherry

Melt the butter in a saucepan, add the mushrooms and pepper and fry gently until soft. Add the flour and cook gently for 1 minute, stirring. Remove the pan from the heat and gradually stir in the milk. Bring to a simmer slowly and continue to cook, stirring constantly, until the sauce thickens. Add the turkey, season to taste with salt, pepper, grated nutmeg and paprika and add the sherry. Heat through, stirring occasionally. Serve with rice or noodles.

Chicken Kiev

4 large chicken breasts, boned and skinned

4 oz. butter, softened

1 tablespoon lemon juice

1 tablespoon fresh parsley, chopped

1 garlic clove, crushed

1 oz. seasoned flour

1 egg, beaten

Fresh white breadcrumbs

Vegetable oil for deep frying

Salt and pepper

Blend the butter with the lemon juice, salt and pepper, parsley and garlic. Beat well together, form into a roll and chill well in the fridge until firm. Place the chicken breasts on a flat surface between sheets of greaseproof paper and pound them to an even thickness with a meat mallet or rolling pin. Cut the butter into four pieces and place one piece on the centre of each chicken breast. Roll up, folding the ends in to enclose the butter completely and secure the rolls with wooden cocktail sticks. Coat each one with the seasoned flour, dip the rolls in the beaten egg and then coat evenly with breadcrumbs. Place the rolls onto a baking sheet and refrigerate for at least 1 hour to allow the coating to dry. In a deep fat fryer, fry the chicken breasts for 12-15 minutes until golden brown and cooked. Taking care not to pierce the breasts, drain well on kitchen paper and serve (remove the cocktail sticks before serving).

Chicken Maryland

8 chicken joints	Fresh breadcrumbs
Seasoned flour	1 oz. butter
1 egg, beaten	Vegetable oil for frying

Coat the chicken joints with seasoned flour, dip in the beaten egg and coat with the breadcrumbs. Refrigerate for at least 1 hour to allow the coating to set. Heat the butter and oil in a large frying pan, add the chicken and fry until lightly browned. Continue frying gently, turning the pieces once, for about 20 minutes, until tender. Alternatively, fry them in a deep fat fryer. Serve the chicken with fried bananas or corn fritters.

Chicken with Pineapple

1 x 3 lb. chicken
1 medium fresh pineapple, peeled, cored and thinly sliced or
1 large tin pineapple slices, drained
2 oz. butter   2 shallots, chopped
Salt and pepper   Watercress to garnish

Separate the skin from the breast of the chicken by inserting your fingers from the neck end and put a slice of pineapple under the skin on each breast. Melt the butter in a roasting tin, add the shallots and cook until softened. Season the chicken with salt and pepper and transfer to a preheated moderately hot oven (400°F or Mark 6). Roast for approx. 1$\frac{1}{2}$ hours. Transfer the chicken to a serving platter and keep hot. Add the remaining pineapple slices to the roasting tin and cook on top of the stove until the pineapple is heated through. Arrange around the chicken and garnish with watercress.

Chicken Chasseur

2 oz. butter   1 x 3 lb. chicken, jointed
6 rindless streaky bacon rashers, cut into large pieces
2 onions, finely chopped   3 tomatoes, skinned and chopped
8 oz. mushrooms, sliced   2 oz. plain flour
1 pint chicken stock   5 fl.oz. dry red wine
2 bay leaves   1 tablespoon soy sauce
Salt and pepper

Melt the butter in a flameproof casserole and fry the chicken pieces with the bacon and onions until the chicken is browned. Sprinkle the flour into the casserole and cook, stirring for 1 minute. Stir in the wine and stock and bring gently to the boil. Add the tomatoes, mushrooms, bay leaves, soy sauce and salt and pepper to taste. Cover the pan and simmer gently for about 1 hour. Remove the bay leaves and check the seasoning before serving.

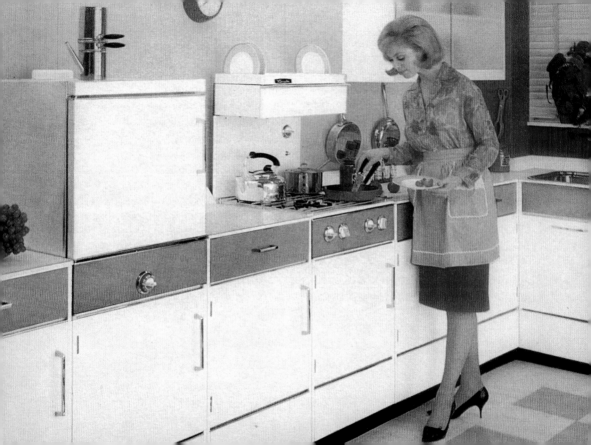

Coronation Chicken

4 lb. cooked chicken   1 tablespoon vegetable oil
1 small onion, finely chopped   1 level tablespoon tomato purée
1 level tablespoon curry paste   4 fl.oz. red wine   1 bay leaf
1 can of apricot halves, drained and puréed
10 fl.oz. mayonnaise   4 fl.oz. whipping cream
Salt and pepper   Watercress   Lemon juice

Heat the oil in a small saucepan, add the onion and cook gently until softened. Add the curry paste, tomato purée, wine, bay leaf and lemon juice. Simmer, uncovered, for about 10 minutes until well reduced. Strain and leave the liquid to cool. Purée the chopped apricot halves in a food processor or through a sieve. Beat the cooled sauce into the mayonnaise with the apricot purée. Whip the cream to stiff peaks and fold into the mixture. Season, adding a little extra lemon juice if necessary. Remove the flesh from the chicken and dice. Fold the chicken pieces into the sauce and garnish with watercress.

Duck with Orange Sauce

4 lb. oven-ready duckling   5 fl.oz. white wine
4 oranges   1 lemon   1 level tbsp sugar
1 tbsp white wine vinegar
2 tbsp brandy (or orange-flavoured liqueur)
1 level tbsp cornflour   1 bunch watercress, to garnish
Salt and pepper

Rub the duck skin with salt and prick the skin all over. Place in the roasting tin with the white wine and roast in the oven at 350°F or Mark 4 for about 2 hours, basting occasionally. Meanwhile, grate the rind from one orange and squeeze the juice from three of the oranges and the lemon. Melt the sugar in a pan with the vinegar and heat until it is a dark brown caramel. Add the brandy and the orange and lemon juice and simmer gently for 5 minutes. When the duck is cooked, remove from the roasting tin and divide into joints. Place the pieces on a serving dish and keep warm. Drain any excess fat from the tin and stir in the cornflour gently until mixed. Add the grated rind and orange sauce, return to the heat and bring gently to the boil, cooking for 2-3 minutes. Season and pour the sauce over the joints. Separate the remaining orange into segments, garnish and serve.

Wiener Schnitzel

4 veal escalopes   1 egg, beaten
5 oz. fresh breadcrumbs   3 oz. butter
8 anchovy fillets, drained
1 egg, hard-boiled and the yolk and white chopped separately
Lemon slices   Salt and pepper

Place each escalope between two sheets of greaseproof paper and flatten thinly. Season the meat on both sides, coat in the beaten egg and dip in the breadcrumbs ensuring it is well covered. Melt the butter in a frying pan and fry the escalopes for 3-5 minutes on each side until golden brown and cooked through. Drain on kitchen paper and keep warm. Serve garnished with the anchovy fillets, chopped egg and lemon slices.

Veal Marsala

2 veal escalopes	Salt
1 oz. butter	Freshly ground black pepper
4 tablespoons Marsala	Lemon slices
1-2 teaspoons lemon juice	Chopped fresh parsley

Trim the veal and season lightly with salt and pepper. Melt the butter in a frying pan and when hot add the escalopes. Cook for 3-4 minutes on each side until lightly browned and almost cooked through. Pour the Marsala over the veal and add the lemon juice and salt and pepper to taste. Carry on cooking gently for a few minutes, turning the veal at least once. Check the seasoning and serve hot, garnished with lemon slices and chopped parsley.

Chilli con Carne

1 lb. minced beef	½ level teaspoon hot chilli powder
1 medium tin red kidney beans	1 level tablespoon flour
1 tablespoon vegetable oil	2 level tablespoon tomato purée
2 medium onions, chopped	2 medium cans chopped tomatoes
1 garlic clove, crushed	Salt and pepper

Heat the oil in a large flameproof pan, add the onions and fry until softened. Add the mince and fry all over until browned. Add the garlic and chilli powder and season to taste. Sprinkle in the flour and stir well. Add the tomato purée and tomatoes with their juice. Bring to the boil and add the kidney beans. Simmer for 30 minutes, stirring occasionally.

Moussaka

2 tablespoons olive oil   1 lb. best lamb mince
1 medium onion, finely chopped   1 large aubergine, sliced thinly
6 oz. mushrooms, chopped   1 clove of garlic, peeled and crushed
2 tablespoons tomato purée   1 tablespoon paprika
½ pint beef stock   Salt and pepper

TOPPING
1 egg   3 oz. Cheddar cheese, grated   5 fl.oz. plain yoghurt

Heat a little of the oil in a large frying pan and fry the aubergine slices in batches on both sides until lightly browned. Set aside the slices. In the remaining oil fry the onion until softened. Add the mince and stir until thoroughly browned on all sides. Stir in the paprika and mix in well, then add the mushrooms, tomato purée, garlic and stock. Season lightly, cover the pan and simmer for about 15-20 minutes. In a greased ovenproof dish place the aubergine slices and meat sauce in alternate layers starting with the sauce and finishing with aubergine. To make the topping, lightly beat the yoghurt with the egg and incorporate the grated cheese. Spread the topping over the moussaka and bake in a preheated oven at 375°F or Mark 5 for about 30-45 minutes. The sauce should be piping hot and the topping nicely browned.

Lasagne

1 lb. green lasagne   12 oz. minced beef
1 small onion   1 stick of celery
1 carrot   1 cup of tomato sauce
4 oz. Reggio Parmesan
Butter, flour and milk to prepare the white sauce
Salt, pepper and extra virgin olive oil, butter

Finely chop the vegetables and lightly fry in extra virgin olive oil, together with the minced meat, the tomato sauce, the salt and pepper. Stir frequently. Meanwhile prepare approx $\frac{1}{2}$ pint of white sauce. When the meat sauce is ready, cook the lasagne in plenty of salted, boiling water. Drain off and place the sheets on a linen cloth. Place a layer of the meat sauce, topped by the white creamed sauce, in a buttered oven dish. Cover with a layer of lasagne and so continue until all the ingredients have been used. Cover with white cream sauce and some flakes of butter and sprinkle with Parmesan. Then cook in the oven at medium heat at a temperature of approx. 325°F or Mark 3 for about 20 minutes until the surface is golden. Serve in the oven dish at the table.

Beef Stroganoff

1½ lb. lean rump or fillet steak, thinly sliced into ¼ x 2 inch strips
3 level tablespoons seasoned flour   2 oz. butter
1 medium onion, thinly sliced   8 oz. mushrooms, sliced
10 fl.oz. soured cream   Salt and pepper

Coat the steak strips with the seasoned flour, then fry in 1 oz. butter for about 6 minutes, until golden brown. Set aside and keep warm. Fry the onion and mushrooms in the remaining butter for 3-4 minutes, season to taste and add the beef. Stir the soured cream into the meat mixture and warm through gently. Serve with noodles or mashed potatoes.

Steak Diane

4 pieces of thin fillet steak
1 oz. butter
1 small onion, very finely chopped

2 tablespoons vegetable oil
2 tablespoons Worcestershire sauce
1 tablespoon lemon juice

1 teaspoon fresh parsley, chopped

Fry the steaks in the butter and oil for 1 to 2 minutes on each side. Remove with a slotted spoon and keep warm. Stir the Worcestershire sauce and lemon juice into the pan juices. Warm through, then add the onion and parsley and cook gently for 2 to 3 minutes until the onion is softened, stirring regularly. Serve the sauce spooned over the steaks.

Beef Provençale

1½ lbs. stewing steak   2 medium carrots, chopped   2 medium onions, sliced
2 cloves of garlic, crushed   3 oz. button mushrooms
1 tin chopped tomatoes   2 rashers streaky bacon, chopped
½ pint red wine   2 tablespoons olive oil   ½ pint beef stock
Bouquet garni   Strip of orange peel
A dozen black olives (pitted)   Salt and pepper
1 tablespoon fresh parsley, chopped

Cut the steak into cubes, place in a large bowl and stir in the wine, olive oil, beef stock and orange peel. Marinate for 2-3 hours. In a heavy bottomed casserole fry the bacon in a little oil, then add the carrots, onions, mushrooms, garlic, parsley and tomatoes. Stir well and cook gently for 10 minutes. Season and then add the meat and marinade and the bouquet garni. Bring to the boil, then cover and cook slowly in a preheated oven at 300°F or Mark 2 for about 3 hours. About half an hour before the end of the cooking time stir in the olives. Remove the bouquet garni and orange peel and serve.

Lemon Meringue Pie

6 oz. shortcrust pastry
FILLING
2 level tablespoons cornflour   4 oz. caster sugar
Grated rind and juice of 2 large lemons
Pinch of ground nutmeg   5 fl.oz. water
2 egg yolks   ½ oz. butter
MERINGUE
2 egg whites   4 oz. caster sugar

Set oven to 375°F or Mark 5. Grease an 8 inch flan tin. Roll out the pastry on a floured surface and use to line the tin. Prick the base and bake blind for 20 to 25 minutes until cooked through. In a bowl, blend the cornflour, sugar, lemon rind and nutmeg with a small amount of the water until smooth. Heat the remaining water in a pan, pour over the blended mixture, return to the pan and cook for one minute, stirring constantly. Allow to cool then mix in the egg yolks, butter and lemon juice and pour into the baked pastry case. MERINGUE: Whip the egg whites until stiff, add half the sugar and beat again. Fold in the remaining sugar and spread over the top of the of the lemon mixture. Bake for 15 to 20 minutes and serve at once. If the pie is to be eaten cold, bake at 325°F or Mark 3 for about 50 to 60 minutes to allow the meringue to harden.

Pineapple Upside-down Pudding

6 oz. butter

7 oz. can pineapple rings, drained

2 glacé cherries, halved

2 oz. soft dark brown sugar

4 oz. caster sugar

2 eggs, beaten

6 oz. self-raising flour

2-3 tbsp pineapple juice

Grease a 7 inch round cake tin and line the base with greaseproof paper. Cream together 2 oz. butter and the brown sugar and spread it over the bottom of the tin. Arrange the pineapple rings and cherries on this layer in the bottom of the tin. Cream together the remaining butter and sugar until pale and fluffy. Add the beaten eggs, a little at a time, beating well. Fold in the flour, adding sufficient pineapple juice to give a dropping consistency, then spread on top of the pineapple rings. Bake in the oven at 350°F or Mark 4 for about 45 minutes. Turn out on to a warmed serving dish and serve. Serves 4.

Crêpes Suzette

8 freshly cooked pancakes   1 oz. caster sugar   2 oz. butter
Finely grated rind and juice of 1 large orange
2 tablespoons orange-flavoured liqueur
3 tablespoons brandy or rum
Cream, to serve

Melt the butter in a large frying pan. Remove from the heat and add the sugar, orange rind and juice and the liqueur. Heat very gently to dissolve the sugar. Fold each pancake in half and then in half again to form a fan shape. Place the pancakes in the frying pan in overlapping lines. Warm the brandy, pour it over the pancakes and set alight. Shake gently, then serve at once with cream.

Lemon Cheesecake

BASE
8 oz. digestive biscuits, crushed
2 oz. butter
2 level tablespoons golden syrup

TOPPING
1 block lemon jelly   Juice and zest of ½ lemon
8 oz. plain cottage cheese, sieved   3 oz. caster sugar
½ pint double cream

Butter a 9 inch flan dish. Put the biscuits into a polythene bag and crush to small crumbs with a rolling pin. Melt the butter in a pan with the syrup and then tip in the crumbs. Remove the pan from the heat and mix together. Tip the mixture into the flan dish, spread out and press down well. Melt the jelly with the smallest amount of boiling water necessary and leave to cool. Grate the lemon zest into a bowl, add the squeezed lemon juice and combine with the jelly. Whisk the cream until stiff, adding the sugar and add to the cottage cheese mix. When the lemon jelly is cool enough, combine it into the cottage cheese mixture. Stir really well together, then spoon the mixture on to the biscuit base and spread out evenly. Put into the refrigerator and leave until set.

Raspberry Ripple Ice Cream

2 oz. flour	1 pint creamy milk
4 egg yolks	½ pint whipping cream
3 oz. caster sugar	8 oz. fresh raspberries
2 teaspoons vanilla extract	2 tablespoons icing sugar

Combine the flour, egg yolks, sugar and vanilla and stir in enough milk to give a thin paste. Heat the remaining milk and gradually stir into the paste, making sure there are no lumps. Pour into a pan and slowly bring to the boil, stirring all the time. Reduce the heat and cook gently for 3 minutes. Remove from the heat, cover with a piece of damp greaseproof paper to prevent a skin forming and leave until cold. Whisk the cream until thick but not stiff and fold into the cold custard. Transfer to a freezerproof container and freeze for 3-4 hours until partly frozen. Sieve the raspberries and stir in the icing sugar. Remove the ice cream from the freezer, beat it well and slightly swirl in the raspberry mixture to give a 'rippled' effect. Return the ice cream to the freezer until solid. Transfer to the refrigerator 20-30 minutes before serving.

Chocolate Roulade

8 oz. caster sugar   6 oz. dark chocolate
5 eggs   3 tablespoons water
10 fl.oz. double cream, lightly whipped

Line a Swiss roll tin with greaseproof paper. Separate the eggs and beat the yolks with the sugar and water. Meanwhile melt the chocolate in a bowl over a pan of hot water on a gentle heat. When melted, add the chocolate to the egg mixture. Whip the egg whites to a firm consistency and gradually fold in gently to the chocolate mixture. Place the mixture in the prepared tin and bake in a preheated oven at 350°F or Mark 4 for 10 to 15 minutes until firm to the touch. Cool, cover with a damp cloth and refrigerate overnight. Turn out onto a board dusted with icing sugar. Remove the greaseproof paper backing. Spread evenly with the whipped cream and roll up. Lift carefully onto a serving dish and dust with icing sugar.

Sherry Trifle

1 lb. fresh raspberries	1 pint custard
1 packet sponge fingers	Raspberry jam
10 fl.oz. whipped cream	Sweet sherry

Flaked almonds

Spread the sponge fingers liberally with raspberry jam and line the base of a glass serving bowl. Spoon the raspberries over the fingers and add sherry to taste, allowing it to soak into the fingers. Pour over the custard and allow to set. Cover with the whipped cream and decorate with flaked almonds. Chill and serve.

METRIC CONVERSIONS

The weights, measures and oven temperatures used in the preceding recipes can be easily converted to their metric equivalents. The conversions listed below are only approximate, having been rounded up or down as may be appropriate.

Weights

Avoirdupois	Metric
1 oz.	just under 30 grams
4 oz. (¼ lb.)	app. 115 grams
8 oz. (½ lb.)	app. 230 grams
1 lb.	454 grams

Liquid Measures

Imperial	Metric
1 tablespoon (liquid only)	20 millilitres
1 fl. oz.	app. 30 millilitres
1 gill (¼ pt.)	app. 145 millilitres
½ pt.	app. 285 millilitres
1 pt.	app. 570 millilitres
1 qt.	app. 1.140 litres

Oven Temperatures

	°Fahrenheit	Gas Mark	°Celsius
Slow	300	2	150
	325	3	170
Moderate	350	4	180
	375	5	190
	400	6	200
Hot	425	7	220
	450	8	230
	475	9	240

Flour as specified in these recipes refers to plain flour unless otherwise described.